Original title:
Life's Meaning Is… Oh Look, a Squirrel

Copyright © 2025 Creative Arts Management OÜ
All rights reserved.

Author: Dean Whitmore
ISBN HARDBACK: 978-1-80566-214-3
ISBN PAPERBACK: 978-1-80566-509-0

The Search for Hidden Treasures

A quest to find the lost delights,
We wander through the sunny heights.
With maps drawn on our eager hearts,
Our laughter echoes, joy imparts.

The treasure chest, a dusty box,
Filled with memories and old socks.
We chase the dreams that twist and fold,
While squirrels giggle, oh so bold.

Ephemeral Glories

A moment shines, then slips away,
Like snacks that vanish after play.
Each giggle bursts like bubblegum,
And squirrels tumble, feeling fun.

The fleeting glories, oh so bright,
We try to catch them, hold them tight.
But when they scatter, what's the fuss?
We'll just make new ones, who can trust?

Nature's Playful Serenade

In parks where critters come alive,
A concert starts, it's time to jive.
With squirrels dancing in a line,
We join the groove, the joy divine.

The trees applaud with rustling leaves,
While sunshine tickles, nature weaves.
A funny tune drifts through the air,
And we just dance without a care.

In the Shade of Uncertainty

Beneath the trees, we scratch our heads,
As questions float like feathered spreads.
What matters most? Who really knows?
Yet, here comes a squirrel, striking poses.

The riddles swirl like summer breeze,
While I trip over roots, oh please!
But laughter bubbles, clears the haze,
As squirrels prance in endless play.

When Time Stands Still

In the park where moments freeze,
A furry friend climbs with ease.
Time takes a break, we grin and stare,
His tiny hops, a dance so rare.

Fingers point, giggles burst loose,
Chasing tails, we find our muse.
The clock forgets to tick away,
In squirrel-filled games, we laugh and play.

The Enchantment of Small Journeys

A stroll beneath the shady trees,
Where squirrels scamper with the breeze.
Tiny explorers, they dart and weave,
In every leap, a magic we believe.

Each nut a treasure, each branch a throne,
With every nibble, they feel at home.
The world is grand when viewed from ground,
As they scurry and chatter, joy is found.

Snapshots of Unheard Tales

Capture moments, don't let them fade,
As little paws make the grandest parade.
In quiet corners, stories unfold,
Whispers of life, adventures untold.

A flick of a tail, a paintbrush created,
Each second remembered, never negated.
Snapshots of chaos, in every nook,
We find ourselves lost in their storybook.

Whimsy Amongst the Twigs

In a world where squirrels reign supreme,
Their silly antics spark a dream.
With laughter echoing beneath the boughs,
Whimsy flourishes, here and now.

They chase the leaves and leap on high,
Bouncing around, like stars in the sky.
In their playful realm, we all belong,
Swaying to the rhythm, life's a song.

In the Wake of Squirrely Adventures

Amidst the trees, a little dance,
Chasing tails with cheeky chance.
Nuts and acorns scatter wide,
In this game, they take great pride.

With beady eyes and quickened feet,
They scurry off, a nimble feat.
Laughter echoes through the park,
As they play until it's dark.

Where Curiosity Leads

With twitching nose and furry coat,
They dart and doddle, then they gloat.
What lies ahead is their great quest,
Each branch and bush, a treasure chest.

The world is big, a puzzling place,
In every nook, a new embrace.
Whiskers twitch with tales to tell,
In their realm, they know it well.

A Moment's Pause

Pause a while, just take it in,
A flash of fur, where have you been?
Nature's jesters, quick to tease,
They seem to do just as they please.

Rest your thoughts, enjoy the sight,
A leap of joy, a sheer delight.
In stillness found, we share a grin,
As squirrels plot their next big win.

Fleeting Glances of Nature's Revelry

In twilight's glow, they frolic free,
A merry flick, a joyful spree.
Nature's jesters at playtime's door,
With every bounce, we love them more.

Their antics filled with boundless cheer,
Each wagging tail, an invitation near.
A moment's joy, a slip, a slide,
With every leap, they dance with pride.

Whimsical Shadows Cross My Path

In the park where laughter flows,
Silly shadows dance and pose.
A fluffy tail, a sudden flare,
Bright-eyed mischief fills the air.

Chasing dreams beneath the trees,
Nature's jest, a breeze of tease.
Squeaky antics, bounding around,
Whiskers twitching on the ground.

The Marvel of Moments Unseen

Hidden gems in every glance,
Life's a skipping, lively dance.
A flash of fur, then gone in a blink,
A perfect way to pause and think.

Magic hides in playful glee,
Noticed mostly by you and me.
Tiny wonders, quick and bright,
Bringing smiles with pure delight.

Tails of Freedom

With every leap, a world unfolds,
A tale of joy that never grows old.
Boundless energy that knows no end,
Chasing shadows, a loyal friend.

Why worry when there's fun to find?
In every scramble, freedom's kind.
A life of nuts and playful spins,
Where every day is where joy begins.

One Nut at a Time

A little treasure hides each day,
In little paws, they scurry away.
Furry thieves with tiny hoards,
Finders keepers, joy aboard!

Nibbles here and munches there,
No cares in the world, just fills the air.
One nut at a time, they scamper and play,
Living in the moment, come what may!

Mischief Among the Roots

Under the oak, a shadow prances,
Tiny paws in wild dances.
Nutty treasures, a hidden stash,
Chasing tails, in a joyous dash.

Leaves rustle, a bond so tight,
Cheeky chitter, morning delight.
Beneath the trees, they play their game,
With nutty zeal, they'll stake their claim.

The Serendipity of Squirrel Flights

Bounding high with leaps of grace,
Chasing sunbeams, a furry race.
A daring dive, into the grass,
With a twitchy tail, they boldly pass.

Each little twist, a joy to see,
Announcing their antics with glee.
Nose to the ground, they scurry and scheme,
Turning the forest into a dream.

Nature's Gentle Invitations

A pause in the path, then a quick glance,
Whiskers twitch in an acorn dance.
Unexpected joys, the branches sway,
Inviting all to join the play.

With every rustle, a chuckle draws,
Nature's charm, without a pause.
Here in the woods, laughter and fun,
In this furry world, we become one.

Unplanned Adventures on a Stroll

Steps in the park, a friendly surprise,
A bushy tail, it catches our eyes.
Darts between trees, quick as a flash,
In these sweet moments, our worries smash.

Impromptu joy from a furry friend,
Chasing light, around the bend.
In the simplest sights, happiness calls,
With a squirrel's grin, the heart enthralls.

Revelations in a Whisk of Fur

In the park where shadows dance,
A furry foe takes a chance.
With acorn dreams in tiny paws,
He scampers quick, without a pause.

A glimpse of joy, a flash of tail,
He weaves a story, never stale.
With antics bold, and small delight,
He turns the mundane into flight.

His little leaps, a joyous spree,
A fleeting jest, pure jubilee.
Oh, how we laugh, oh, how we play,
As nature spins in her own way.

Capturing Fleeting Whispers of Joy.

In a sunbeam, he's a blur,
Chasing shadows, leaves and fur.
What secrets hide in nature's hug?
With a twitchy nose and a little shrug.

Around the tree, he makes his dash,
A living blur, a fuzzy flash.
He pauses just to steal a glance,
And off he goes, what a prance!

We sigh and chuckle at his charms,
With tiny feet that weave like yarns.
Oh, pesky spirit, do return,
And teach us how to laugh and learn.

The Essence of Fleeting Moments

Upon a branch, the world extends,
A spirit frolics as he bends.
His agile dance, a playful tease,
Life's tapestry blown in the breeze.

With wide-eyed glee, he leaps around,
A jester's crown in nature found.
He scampers high, then swoops back low,
Forget the world, just watch him go!

Moments like this can often fade,
Yet in his grace, a joy cascades.
Unruly joy in nature's scheme,
A furry vault, a happy dream.

Whispers of Fluffy Tails

With fluffy tails that dance and sway,
He hops and skips to greet the day.
A sneaky glance over leafy greens,
In his small world, magic beams.

His whiskered face, a curious sight,
Eyes sparkling with playful light.
The world can wait, the world can spin,
But here, we'll laugh, let the fun begin!

Moments scattered, like fallen leaves,
Through laughter, our spirit weaves.
In this ruckus, a truth unfolds,
Joy's in the small things, as life unfolds.

A Glimpse into Existence

In the park, a flash, a blur,
A tiny creature, a furry fur.
It leaps and bounds, so full of glee,
What fun it is, oh look and see!

Thoughts of grandeur, deep and wide,
Quickly lost on this fleeting ride.
Chasing tails, both nuts and dreams,
In laughter's echo, nothing's as it seems.

A moment captured, a fleeting glance,
In antics wild, we find our dance.
With every hop, a chuckle helps,
Forget your worries, laugh with elves!

For meaning hides in laughter bright,
When joy's so clear, what's wrong feels right.
Just follow that fluff, wherever it goes,
In simple moments, the joy bestows.

The Dance of Unforeseen Joys

A jig in the grass, a flick of a tail,
Suddenly my thoughts start to sail.
What was I saying? Oh, what a bore!
Look at that rascal, what a grand score!

Around the tree, with pirouettes bold,
Every leap tells a story untold.
I laugh out loud, my worries dissipate,
As chuckles chase after its playful gait.

When purpose looms heavy, with serious weight,
A fuzzy interloper seems to create.
It's all so silly, yet perfectly right,
In every distraction, there shines a light.

So dance, little critter, keep spinning around,
In this circus of life, joy's always found.
With every mishap, we learn and we play,
The art of distraction brightens the day.

In Pursuit of Nutty Secrets

Whiskers twitching, a sudden stop,
What's that hiding? Is it a prop?
Under the leaves, the quest begins,
With every search, excitement wins.

A treasure trove of dreams to race,
In every nook, a secret place.
Finding nuggets of laughter and cheer,
For nutty secrets, we persevere.

Oh, look! A flicker, it scurries away,
What have I lost? Was it my play?
Life's little puzzles, spicy and sweet,
All roll together, a funny treat.

With tiny paws, clumsy yet swift,
In chasing the secrets, we all get a lift.
So pause for a moment, and join the quest,
In searching for joy, we surely are blessed.

When Distraction Strikes

At the corner of focus, a flicker appears,
Distraction dances, winking in cheers.
Oh, important thoughts? They waltz out the door,
Chasing that fluff is what we adore!

The mind plays tricks, a playful duel,
When squirrels hijack, reason's a fool.
"Was I making dinner or writing a song?"
Now giggles erupt, and it won't take long.

Joy strikes the heart, from whimsy's embrace,
In this madcap chase, I find my place.
So here's to the chaos, the fun and delight,
When distraction strikes, it feels so right.

In every nut, a fragment of cheer,
Taking a minute to laugh and to leer.
So let's all wander where squirrels might run,
In the playful breeze, we'll follow the fun!

Unexpected Intermissions

In the middle of a serious chat,
A fluffy tail zooms right past.
Thoughts of wisdom suddenly scatter,
As curious furballs steal the master.

Plans laid out for the big day,
Interrupted by a squirrel's play.
With every leap, we lose our thought,
To nature's antics we are caught.

Dishes piled, chores in demand,
Yet the squirrel performs, oh so grand!
Cacophony of giggles fills the air,
As we forget life's serious glare.

Living for the now, we find,
In furry friends that run and unwind.
In the chaos, laughter finds a way,
An unexpected pause in our weekday.

The Spirit of Discovery

Around the bend, there's a rustle,
A glimpse of mischief causes a tussle.
Forget the maps and grand old themes,
For the real treasure lies in playful dreams.

Magnifying glass won't do,
When a nutter dances, it's a view!
Chasing shadows, through leaves they skitter,
In their antics, our worries wither.

Oh, how they dart, quick and spry,
Moments like these just fly by.
In the quest for snacks, there's no end,
Squirrels, oh squirrels, our joy they send.

Exploring corners where laughter blooms,
With every hop, out humor zooms.
So let's embrace silliness around,
For in their chase, pure joy is found!

An Afternoon of Acorn Dreams

In the park where laughter rings,
Acorns fall like nature's blings.
A jumping jester steals the show,
As our hearts lift, worries go below.

Daydreams danced under the trees,
Where fretful thoughts vanish with ease.
With each chitter, life feels right,
Acorns drop in the dappled light.

Pine cones tumble, a subtle crash,
As squirrels gather, oh what a stash!
In their world, we wish to play,
An afternoon of color, bright and gay.

So let's reminisce with grand delight,
Embracing chaos, laughing in light.
For every acorn is a gleam,
In our hearts, we chase that dream.

Curiosity Unleashed

With every twitch of a furry tail,
Curiosity whispers, never frail.
Bushy brows and twitching nose,
In this wild dance, our laughter grows.

On branches high, they plot their course,
Defying gravity with a little force.
A nutty pursuit, a playful spree,
As we chuckle, they shine with glee.

Silly antics, a hop and jump,
With every surprise, we feel the thump.
From tree to tree, the world's a treat,
In their play, we find our beat.

So follow the chase, let it unfold,
In whimsy's grip, our hearts feel bold.
For in the chaos of silly spree,
We discover joy, wild and free.

The Glee of Curiosity Roused

In the park where laughter reigns,
A little critter bounds and gains.
Its twitchy tail, so full of glee,
Distracts us all, just watch and see.

With each leap, a question springs,
What joy the searching spirit brings!
Nutty treasures hide and play,
While giggles chase the blues away.

Chasing shadows, near and far,
A game unfolds beneath the star.
With every rustle, hearts do race,
In this delightful, silly chase.

So pause and grin, let worries go,
For laughter's found in antics low.
Inquiring minds, oh what a thrill,
Just like a squirrel, we seek that skill.

A Squirrel's Dream: A Tale of Smallness

Once upon a branch so high,
A tiny dreamer danced and spry.
Fluffy tails and visions bright,
In search of snacks by morning light.

Around the roots, the antics bloom,
With acorns piled in a cozy room.
The world, it seems, is vast yet small,
As laughter echoes, a sweet call.

With each bound, the spirit sings,
Delightful chaos that nature brings.
Oh, the wonders just within reach,
Cheerful lessons, life's true speech.

So join the dance, embrace the play,
A lesson learned in every sway.
For tiny dreams can steal the show,
In strange corners, oh, how they grow!

Shadows of Serendipity

In dappled light, a shadow flits,
A furry friend with playful wits.
A hop, a leap, a sudden stop,
Serendipity's merry drop.

With twinkling eyes, this charmer grins,
As chaos sparked, adventure spins.
Through whispered leaves, it scampers fast,
Each glance, a giggle from the past.

Moments lost in fleeting chase,
Absurdity's the perfect place.
Between the boughs, life's secrets swirl,
In every dash, a vibrant twirl.

So let us wander, embrace the fall,
For in these shadows, we stand tall.
With every skip, we come to find,
Joy's hidden magic lingers behind.

Detours of Delight

On winding paths where giggles roam,
A squirrel plots its happy home.
With every twist, a chuckle grows,
Among the trees, oh how it flows!

Bouncing here and circling there,
Not a rush, just playful air.
In every nook, a silly sight,
Turns mundane strolls to pure delight.

The world unfolds, a curious quest,
In nutty mischief, we find our best.
With laughter blazing like the sun,
Life's tangled routes, oh, they are fun!

So take the plunge, embrace surprise,
In every corner, wonder lies.
For detours lead to laughter's call,
In playful threads, we find it all.

In the Wake of Curious Souls

In the park where thoughts drift free,
A flash of fur, oh joy to see!
Nuts and twirls, tiny acrobat,
While we ponder where we're at.

Philosophers with coffee cups,
Debating meanings, spilling up.
But what's the sense in all this talk?
When a nut is found, just take a walk!

Around the trees, they leap and dive,
In their world, they truly thrive.
With each bound, they steal our frowns,
A majestic dance in leafy crowns.

So let's forget the serious chase,
And join the quest in this furry race.
In the chase of critters, joy unfurls,
As laughter stirs in a whirl of swirls.

Small Wonders in a Big World

A whiskered face, two bright eyes beam,
In a world that feels like a grand dream.
Chasing shadows, dodging trees,
Unraveling with comical ease.

We walk in circles, scratch our heads,
While little ones launch from their beds.
What's deep and profound can wait for noon,
As we marvel at their daring swoon.

Each stuttered step has its own glee,
Who's the wise one? You or me?
As we chase the giggles in the dew,
Each petal glitters with joy brand new.

In our quest for wisdom, let's pause and cheer,
For small delights draw us near.
When the world feels heavy, just take a look,
At the playful dance in every nook.

Epiphany at the Edge of a Tree

At the base of a mighty oak,
We ponder and talk, till we choke.
Then comes a scurry, a blink so quick,
A furry philosopher with a clever trick.

Was that a revelation? Or just a tail?
As wisdom slips, like wind in a sail.
Staring at splendor, lost in the view,
Nature's jesters make old thoughts feel new.

They climb with purpose, they leap with flair,
While we are tethered to our heavy chair.
In the antics of life, there lies the clue,
Joy is weaving, ever so true.

Beneath the branches, we seek the wise,
In the rustle of leaves, a small surprise.
Perhaps it's simpler to just be free,
And laugh as we find what matters to thee.

The Flicker of a Tiny Spirit

Bright-eyed wanderer, what will you find?
In the quiet moments, you've left us blind.
With every shuffle, you steal a heart,
In your tiny dance, you play your part.

On a quest for acorns, you dash and zoom,
In your vibrant world, there's always room.
We ponder fate, you ponder lunch,
In the tales of swirling leaves, we all hunch.

Little creature with a mission so grand,
You teach us all to just understand.
That laughter rises in the smallest things,
As your frolic reminds us of joys it brings.

So let's drop the gravity of heavy thoughts,
Embrace the whimsy that your soul spots.
For in your spirit, bright and spry,
We catch a glimpse of joy flying by.

The Art of Noticing

A rustle here, a twitchy tail,
A flash of fur, where did it sail?
Pondering thoughts of deep, grand quests,
But wait! There's something that's far more jest.

We chase the big, the profound sights,
Yet often miss the silly delights.
In branches high or on the ground,
Joy gin on wonder that can astound.

And if you stop to have a peek,
There's magic in the small and meek.
While seeking truths of grand events,
You'll find them hiding behind tall fence.

So here's a tip from wise old me,
Keep your eyes peeled for frolic and spree.
In every corner of trivial bliss,
A quirky pause is worth the miss.

Breathless Discovery

Running fast, a dash of fur,
Hanging onto nature's blur.
In a chaotic burst of zest,
Chasing dreams, you'd never guess.

Through branches tangled, jumps and twirls,
A happy dance as the world unfurls.
We hustle hard, we strive and race,
Yet silly sights put smiles in place.

Fleeting moments, oh so rare,
A squirrel's pause, a silly stare.
With cheeky grins, it steals the scene,
Who knew that snack could be a queen?

So live your days with laughter's lens,
Forget the worries; make new friends.
In nature's antics, joy's released,
Those breathless moments should never cease.

Enigmas of Everyday Encounters

What's that twitch? A little tease,
A riddle wrapped in leaves and trees.
Ponder the world, but don't just brood,
Fun can hide where it's most shrewd.

Questions spin in endless ways,
As squirrels dart, or sunbeams blaze.
Do we really know what it means,
When nature laughs in subtle scenes?

In mundane hours, discovery calls,
Every glance could lead to sprawl.
Unravel laughter in your day,
Surprise awaits in cheeky play.

The chase for truths, we all embark,
Yet humor hides where life leaves a mark.
Embrace the fumbles and the cheer,
For every mystery brings delight near.

When Curiosity Calls

Tap-tap, what's that? Come see, my friends,
Curiosity's call, it never ends.
A twitch of paws, a playful glance,
In every moment, a chance to dance.

Wander far, don't stay confined,
The world's absurdity keeps us aligned.
Adventure waits, so take a cue,
And find the humor in all that's new.

With every creature, big or small,
Life's bright jests are open for all.
A cheeky grin, a squirrel so spry,
Whispers that laughter will never die.

So heed the call, embrace the fun,
In chasing joy, we'll never run.
For when we notice the silly things,
We find the joy that laughing brings.

Unraveling Life's Quirks

In a park where thoughts go to play,
A furry friend steals the day.
Chasing shadows, avoiding the fuss,
Nature's own little comic bus.

With a rustle and twitch, they prance,
Inviting us to join the dance.
Nibbling acorns with such delight,
Oh, the joys of a simple sight!

A leap and a bound, a mischievous turn,
In their antics, our worries burn.
What a lesson from tiny paws,
To find humor in nature's laws.

So let's embrace the little things,
To joy and laughter, the heart sings.
For in a world too often serious,
It's the small quirks that make us curious.

The Laughter of Small Creatures

Squirrels scamper, like tiny clowns,
In their antics, we cast off frowns.
Flipping and flopping, a wild spree,
Who knew joy could come so carefree?

With twitching tails and beady eyes,
They put on shows, oh what a surprise!
Nuts are their treasure, a silly quest,
In their world, they're truly blessed!

Each jump is a giggle, each hop a cheer,
In the chaos, the meaning is clear!
For when we watch them play about,
The weight of the world starts to pout.

Join the fun, let worries flee,
Take a cue from the jubilee.
For life's laughter is often near,
In the smallest moments, loud and clear.

Threads of Adventure Unspooled

With a dash and a dart, they weave through the trees,
Explorers with tails, in the gentle breeze.
Each nut they bury, a map to delight,
Whiskers twitching, oh what a sight!

Dancing in circles, they call to the sky,
Chasing their dreams, oh how they fly!
Nature's own jesters, with mischief afoot,
In their chaotic ballet, nothing is moot!

Every flick of their ear, a story to tell,
In the woods where they laugh, all is well.
Lessons in fluff and little surprises,
The treasure of playtime loudly rises.

So we follow their trails, through laughter and play,
Chasing our thoughts, letting them stray.
For adventure awaits in the wild and the fun,
With each tiny creature, our hearts become one.

Finding Delight in the Mundane

Amidst the sneakers and rustling leaves,
In the simplest acts, joy oft cleaves.
A curious head pokes from a tree,
Oh, what a silly little spree!

In a world that rushes, hear the cheer,
When fluff-footed friends come so near.
Their dashes and leaps are a grand parade,
Finding smile-drops in the charade.

Every moment spent in their tiny grace,
Reminds us to cherish each little space.
For in the ordinary, magic will sing,
As we watch what the tiny creatures bring.

So pause for a second, just take a look,
New joy is waiting, like a fine book.
Embrace the laughter, the silliness too,
In the dance of the mundane, find something new!

Capturing the Here and Now

In the garden, we roam, bright day,
Chasing shadows, come what may.
Sudden movements, quick and spry,
What's that? A critter! Zooming by.

Time slips through fingers, can't hold tight,
Joyful moments dance in light.
Oh, to be quick, to jump and play,
What fun to see it bound away.

The chatter of the world grows small,
With every leap, I catch my fall.
Giggling wildly, I laugh aloud,
As nature's secrets, I dare to sound.

Ponder not too deeply, just give chase,
In every rustle, find your place.
With silly grins and a heart so free,
Even a squirrel brings joy to me!

Unexpected Revelations in Nature's Kingdom

Underneath the shade so wide,
A furry friend makes quite the glide.
It scrambles up, not hard to spot,
Who knew nature could be so hot?

Thoughts of wisdom, they take flight,
When a bushy tail gives fright.
In the quiet, laughs emerge,
A glimpse of fun—a serendipity surge!

Life's a riddle, a playful jest,
Where sneaky critters put minds to test.
With every hop, a giggle rings,
Nature's tricks are wondrous things.

Not pondering deep, just soaking in,
Moments fleeting, let the joy begin.
Under leaves where laughter swells,
Each little leap—oh, what it tells!

Hide and Seek with Existence

Behind the tree, what do I see?
A tiny flicker, could it be?
With wiggly whiskers and mischievous eyes,
My fleeting thoughts begin to rise.

Around I spin, in wonderment,
As sassy bounds—what a quick ascent!
Who hides here, beneath the boughs?
A game of peek-a-boo, I bow.

Catching glimpses, I chase and twirl,
In my head, thoughts begin to swirl.
Questions echo but find no sound,
As I leap and laugh on leafy ground.

Time slips softly, unnoticed by me,
Lost in frolic, my heart feels free.
With giggles bright, I seek once more,
In this lively game, who keeps the score?

Whimsy Amongst the Leaves

Dancing sunlight, shadows play,
Amidst the trees, I drift away.
A flick of fur, a flick of tail,
What's this creature? Oh, it won't fail!

Golden acorns and frothy green,
A secret world, a lively scene.
Skip and hop, the fun's not done,
In this wild chase, I'm on the run!

Nature chuckles, just look and see,
A playful pause, invites to be.
Amidst the laughter, a chorus sings,
A squirrel's antics—oh, the joy it brings!

Suddenly, life seems rich and bright,
With each small twist, pure delight.
So chase the moment, feel the breeze,
Whimsy thrives in swaying leaves!

Glimpses of Magic in Everyday Life

In a world where wonders play,
A kitten pounces in the fray.
A coffee spill, a dance so wild,
Oh look! It's chaos, just a child.

A rainbow forms from garden hoses,
While ants march on with tiny poses.
The mailman trips, a parcel flies,
Oh look! A squirrel in disguise!

A puddle gleams with skies of blue,
While ducks are quacking, oh what's new!
A paper plane, it sails so high,
Oh look! A cloud that says goodbye.

In shadows long, the echoes play,
Mismatched socks on laundry day.
The world spins on with giggles bright,
Oh look! It's joy that takes flight.

Hidden Treasures in the Woodlands

In the forest deep, a secret lies,
A shiny rock that catches eyes.
The rustle of leaves, a snicker's sound,
Oh look! It's magic all around.

A bubble wand that's lost its charm,
While frolicking frogs raise alarm.
A twist of fate, a silly breeze,
Oh look! A squirrel stealing cheese!

Wildflowers bloom with colors bright,
As squirrels dance in pure delight.
A treasure hunt, your heart will leap,
Oh look! The world is yours to keep.

In whispers low, the trees do speak,
With hidden paths that play hide and seek.
An acorn rolls, it's quite a show,
Oh look! A friend you didn't know.

Ribbons of Laughter under the Oak

Under the oak, where shadows sway,
A squirrel prances, bright and gay.
With ribbons tossed and giggles shared,
Oh look! A day that blushed and dared.

A picnic spread, a madcap feast,
The ants march in, they're quite a beast.
Cookies crumble, laughter flies,
Oh look! Those pies, oh how they rise!

A breeze that plays with hats and hair,
As old folks dance without a care.
The sunny patch, a lazy spot,
Oh look! Who knew fun could be caught?

With every turn, a new delight,
As nature beckons, bold and bright.
With fabric dreams and endless play,
Oh look! We found our hearts today.

A Mosaic of Tiny Wonders

Tiny adventures, big surprise,
Bubbles float up to the skies.
A pebble chat, a breezy friend,
Oh look! The fun that won't end.

Insects march with little feet,
As children laugh and dance to beat.
Each treasure found along the trail,
Oh look! It's magic without fail.

Leaves that whisper secrets low,
While wobbly ships in puddles flow.
A playful tug, a jacket flies,
Oh look! The world is full of ties.

With every glance, a story spun,
In tiny moments, we find the fun.
A patchwork life, so full and bright,
Oh look! We laugh until the night.

A World Awaits in Silent Glances

In the park, all seems still,
But there's mischief by the hill.
With twitching tails and bulging cheeks,
Silent glances hide their sneaks.

Like little ghosts they dart about,
Chasing dreams with squeaky shouts.
Forgotten plans, and lunch ungraced,
In this chase, silence's replaced.

Watch closely, oh what a show,
Nature's jesters steal the glow.
With each skip and hop, they plot,
Life's humor brews in every spot.

We laugh and cheer their wild parade,
While munching snacks that we have laid.
In this frenzy, joy takes flight,
With every leap, our hearts feel light.

Sprightly Shenanigans Beneath the Canopy

Beneath the leaves, a dance unfolds,
A jumpy troop, so brave and bold.
With every leap, a giggling sound,
Their silly antics know no bound.

Peeking from behind the trees,
They frolic with the buzzing bees.
A branch too low, a daring bound,
Oops! Down they go without a sound.

Little acorns thrown about,
In their tussles, joy's devout.
A peek-a-boo here, a scamper there,
With the wind, their secrets share.

How can we not join the fun?
Their laughter shines like morning sun.
In every twist, a chance to grin,
Join the dance; let joy begin!

The Elusive Joys of the Unexpected

Oh, what joy, a sudden flash!
A furry friend in nimble dash.
From branches high to ground below,
In playful leaps, their mischief grows.

With acorns rolling, they engage,
A comic ballet, the latest stage.
Will they trip, or soar with grace?
In this showdown, smiles interlace.

We stand amazed, hearts afire,
At tiny tricks that never tire.
Every stumble, a giggle shared,
In this moment, nothing's spared.

As twilight drapes the world in gold,
The tales of their antics are retold.
In furry chaos, we find we thrive,
Through innocent glee, we feel alive.

Unexpected Visitors in the Sunlight

Under the sun, a sudden spark,
A tiny buzz, a merry lark.
With sudden skits and faux pas grand,
They prance about, each acorn planned.

From shadows deep, they leap and play,
Chasing light through the bright bouquet.
Laughter echoes, what a delight!
Watch them twirl, a comical sight.

When snacks are dropped, it's quite the show,
With feasting antics sure to grow.
Their little armies march in line,
In happy chaos, they all dine.

So let's sit back, enjoy the fun,
As shadows stretch and day is done.
In every whirl and zany twirl,
These little moments, oh what a pearl!

When Wonder Meets the Ordinary

In the park, the sun is bright,
A whiskered friend darts out of sight.
With a twitch and a bound, it steals the show,
While we marvel, 'Where did it go?'

A simple stroll turns into a chase,
A furry blur in the open space.
With laughter shared and eyes wide,
Nature's charm, our hearts are tied.

What's this life, just a stroll and sigh?
Or magic hidden in a tiny guy?
We search for truth in the mundane,
As this little nutter brings us gain.

Moments fade, while antics spin,
Who knew fun could stem from within?
With every leap, the world's a stage,
Squirrels in charge, we turn the page.

The Joy of Small Discoveries

A stroll through grass, all is still,
Then a flash of fur gives us a thrill.
Chasing acorns, with goofy grace,
   Bringing smiles to every face.

Beneath the trees, the laughter rings,
A little creature, oh what fun it brings!
Small moments, like seeds, they grow,
   In our hearts, the joy we sow.

What's that up there, a bright-eyed tease?
   Climbing high with such ease!
   Each tiny treasure, a tiny thrill,
In nature's game, we find our will.

So stop and stare, embrace the fun,
Life's little wonders have just begun.
   In silly antics, truth we'll find,
In those small moments, we are aligned.

Sparkling Eyes under Rustling Leaves

Under the branches, we stop to play,
A shimmering glance cuts through the day.
With sparkling eyes, and tails that twirl,
Nature does its own little whirl.

Among the leaves, a rustling throng,
Tiny paws scamper; it feels so wrong!
Yet laughter erupts from the ground below,
As furry tornadoes steal the show.

What are we seeking, wisdom or cheer?
When squirrels parade, it's perfectly clear.
Nature's wonders are not so far,
In each little fluff, we find a star!

So as we shuffle through wood and glen,
A laugh, a chase, we learn again.
In every leap, the ordinary sings,
As joyful laughter on tiny wings.

Nature's Playful Interruption

Out for a jog, head in the zone,
Yet a fuzzy bandit makes my heart moan.
With a dash and a leap, it claims the trail,
In this simple moment, my worries pale.

What chaos reigns in a forest green,
Where a tiny creature holds the scene.
Dancing through the brush with glee,
Reminding me to just be free.

Each darty step, like a little jig,
I laugh at the antics, both bold and big.
In its playful world, everything's right,
As I chase shadows, my heart takes flight.

So take a pause, for joy comes swift,
In nature's quirks, we find our gift.
With squirrels leading, come join the fun,
In every moment, there's joy to be spun.

Threads of Fauna in Our Fabric

In a tapestry of days, we weave,
A tiny creature darts, hard to believe.
With fluffy tail and playful bounds,
In the chaos, joy is found.

Amid the tasks, a sudden pause,
Nature's jester, with no cause.
A twitch, a leap, away it goes,
In a moment, laughter grows.

Stitching colors in our veins,
Each furry friend can break the chains.
What are worries when they play?
A bright distraction leads the way.

So let the threads of fauna weave,
A story that we all can cleave.
For in the chaos, we might see,
The joy that waits, wild and free.

The Unexpected Symphony of Nature

A rustle here, a chirp up there,
A melody spins through the air.
Each creature plays its joyful note,
Nature's song makes hearts float.

Just when you think the world is still,
A furry artist brings the thrill.
Chasing shadows, bold and spry,
Setting rhythms for the eye.

With every leap, a joyful tune,
A dance beneath the smiling moon.
Oh, how the song begins to swell,
Each note a giggle, can't you tell?

In every sound, a comic twist,
A symphony that can't be missed.
So let the world around us play,
With critters leading the ballet.

Embracing Distraction

Oh look! A movement by the tree,
A furry fellow, wild and free.
In the midst of daily grind,
A furry friend, race unconfined.

Tasks can wait, just for a while,
Watch him scamper, then smile.
Chasing dreams can be absurd,
When joy appears, it's never blurred.

The clock ticks on, but pause is right,
In every whim, there's pure delight.
A twist of fate, a playful dance,
Life shines bright in every glance.

So embrace that fleeting sight,
Let the world spark sheer delight.
For in distraction, we may find,
A treasure waiting, one of a kind.

A Nutshell of Existence

In a world that sometimes seems so bland,
A curious creature runs through the land.
With every pebble, it starts to whirl,
Like the plot of a novel that begins to unfurl.

What is this thing we call our quest?
Perhaps it's buried in a squirrel's jest.
A simple chase, a joyful spin,
Each tiny moment, let happiness in.

With every nut, there's a small delight,
A treasure hoard beneath the light.
No grand design, just playful fun,
Life's kernel whispers, "You've just begun."

So fill your days with laughter and play,
Let each adventure carry you away.
For in this nutshell, truth might show,
The joy of living, a vibrant glow.

Stories Beneath the Canopy

In sunlight's dance on leafy floors,
Curious critters peek out from doors.
A flick of a tail, a quick little scamper,
Oh, did you see? Was that a champer?

Amidst the whispers of branches slight,
A gathering of giggles in morning light.
Chasing shadows, in playful spree,
Wait, what's that? No, just a tree!

With every rustle a tale unfolds,
From bunnies to birds, their antics bold.
A chirp, a cheer, a soft little zing,
Oh, look! A squirrel—what joy you bring!

So here we sit, with laughter so bright,
In nature's booth, oh what a sight!
Seeking joy, with spirits so spry,
Under the canopy, we laugh and sigh.

The Art of Wonderment

Amidst the clutter of daily grind,
A dash of whimsy is what we find.
With eyes wide open, we pause to stare,
Oh, look! A squirrel climbing there!

A twirl of leaves, a jump, a skip,
Nature's antics make our hearts flip.
From wiggly worms to skippity frogs,
Every moment's magic in smiles and logs.

The mystery lies in each fleeting glance,
A reflective pause, a serendipitous chance.
Laughter erupts from the simplest play,
As nature's jesters come out to play!

So raise a cheer for the sights we see,
From buzzing bees to the tallest tree.
In this grand circus, we all take part,
With each little creature, it warms the heart.

A Tapestry of Little Moments

In the garden of giggles, the laughter blooms,
Petals unfolding in soft wondrous rooms.
A flick of a paw, from the bushes it darts,
Oh look! A squirrel, it steals our hearts!

With a twitch of its nose and a playful glance,
We're swept in a whirlwind, we can't help but dance.
A blurt of delight in the canopy's shade,
As scenes of delight begin to parade.

Each twist and turn, a whimsical sight,
Moments unraveling, pure delight.
From sunlight's kiss to shadows that blend,
Ah, the smiles that nature's moments send.

So let's weave the tales, from beginning to end,
Of frolicking friends and the joy they send.
In the quiet spaces, let giggles unfurl,
As we pause for a moment to watch a squirrel.

Nature's Interruptions

In the midst of chores, a flash catches our eyes,
Nature's performers, oh, what a surprise!
With tails a-wagging, and whiskers in play,
Oh look! A squirrel, come join the fray!

As we fetch the mail, or cook up a feast,
Squirrels provide humor, from greatest to least.
A tumble, a roll, a dramatic charade,
The ultimate jesters, all unafraid!

From dazzling dives to the top of a tree,
Nature's disruptors bring pure glee.
With every distraction, a chuckle bestowed,
A reminder that joy is an endless road.

So here's to the pauses, the silly delights,
In garden and park, in days and in nights.
With laughter in tow, and hearts all a-whirl,
Enjoying the whimsy that comes from a squirrel!

In Search of the Wonder Within

With twinkling eyes, I roam around,
Chasing shadows, laughter bound.
Every corner whispers fun,
Squirrels dance beneath the sun.

A twist, a turn, a playful chase,
Nature's joy, a smiling face.
Forget the world, just run and play,
Magic hides in just one sway.

The trees appear to wiggle, grin,
While furry friends dart from within.
A hop, a skip, then off they flee,
Oh, what a thrill it is to see!

So pause and watch the tale unfold,
In every leap, a joy untold.
Among the branches, giggles ring,
Life's a circus; come, join the fling.

The Art of Losing Oneself in Nature

Wander deep through leafy groves,
Where laughter plays and mischief roves.
A glimpse of fur, a twitch of tail,
Nature's jesters never fail.

With every rustle and gentle thump,
A secret joke makes my heart jump.
Forget the path, just follow glee,
In nature's realm, I'm wild and free.

Each bead of dew, a twinkling jest,
Moments passed that feel like a fest.
Who needs a plan or grand design?
Just dancing squirrels and a good time!

So chase the whimsy, let it flow,
Adventure waits where squirrels go.
In their frolic, I find delight,
In every chase, the world feels right.

Secrets in the Rustling Underbrush

In tangled leaves, whispers creep,
Squirrels giggle, secrets they keep.
With every shadow, stories hide,
Nature's jest, our cheerful guide.

Branches sway as if to tease,
A playful breeze among the trees.
What's that sound? Oh, just a show,
A tiny leap from below!

Among the ferns, joy's alive,
Life tumbles forth, a happy drive.
Who knew the forest could be such fun,
With every rustle, new stories spun?

So take a moment, breathe it in,
In nature's game, we all can win.
With every giggle, with every dash,
We find our truths in nature's splash.

Enchantment Found in a Tiny Leap

A twitch of tail, a playful bounce,
With every jump, my heart does flounce.
Through sunlit paths and shade's retreat,
Squirrels' antics can't be beat.

They leap like they know some secret rhyme,
In every bound, they steal the time.
What's life but joy in such a race?
Each fleeting gust, a warm embrace.

Snickers echo through the trees,
As nature hums with whispered tease.
Oh look, another daring twist,
How can I help but feel this bliss?

So join the dance, let laughter swell,
In every bound, we find our spell.
The world's a stage; come take a leap,
Embrace the joy that life can keep.

Mischief in the Meadow

In the field where daisies sway,
A tiny creature starts to play.
With a twitching tail and cheeky grin,
Life's a game, let the fun begin!

Chasing shadows, hopping about,
Who knew chaos could lead to a rout?
Poking noses in all the wrong places,
It's laughter that fills all the spaces!

Every flip and every twirl,
A furry little bundle, what a whirl!
As the sun dips low in the sky,
We watch this rascal as time flies by.

In the meadow where giggles bloom,
You find joy, dispelling gloom.
With every leap, every bound,
Mischief dances all around!

Moments of Marvel Amidst Chaos

In the midst of daily hustle,
A rascal stirs up quite the tussle.
With a clever dash and a quick little flip,
You can't help but chuckle at the trip!

Amidst the clutter, a pause for cheer,
As mischief reigns, far from fear.
Laughter bubbles when chaos takes hold,
In the heart of mayhem, stories unfold.

Sneaking snacks, oh what a sight,
Tiny paws feeling just right!
A dash of joy in the afternoon sun,
Moments like these, oh what fun!

So kick back and join in the spree,
Life's quirks are best when shared carefree.
In the chaos, find joy to embrace,
With marbles and friends, a wild race!

Adventures in a Backyard Realm

In the backyard, the world feels wide,
With tiny feet, treasures to hide.
A quest for snacks beneath the trees,
Adventures bloom with every breeze.

A dig here, a nibble there,
With giggles echoing everywhere.
What's that noise? Oh, it's just fun!
A game with shadows, the day's not done!

Jumping over pots and twigs galore,
Chasing dreams and maybe more.
In this realm of green and cheer,
Every corner has something clear.

Shiny trinkets caught in sight,
Moments sparkled, oh so bright!
An unexpected twist on every path,
In this wild story, love's the math!

The Joy of Unexpected Detours

A stroll through the park, a simple thought,
But hey, look there! A feast just caught!
With curious eyes and a dashing dash,
Sudden surprises, a whimsical splash.

Every moment teases with delight,
Winding paths that dance in light.
Who knew the day would twist and twirl?
With every corner, a giggle unfurl!

From acorns to whispers, nature's call,
In the grand design, we're having a ball.
What's the point? Who cares, you see?
It's the surprises that bring glee!

So chase the whims that lead astray,
Life's riddles can lighten the day.
With each turn, let laughter flow,
Unexpected joys in the ebb and flow!

Transitory Wonders Unveiled

Little things dance in the breeze,
A flash of fur with nimble ease.
While we ponder deep and long,
Nature reminds us where we belong.

With acorns stashed and eyes so bright,
A moment shared brings pure delight.
To chase the shadows and leap so high,
We smile at the antics zipping by.

In fleeting glances, joy's revealed,
Through furry friends, the heart is healed.
A skip, a hop, they dart from view,
In chaos, find your laughter true.

So pause amidst the daily grind,
Uncover treasures, joys to find.
In their frolic, lessons be,
Simple wonders, wild and free.

Life on a Limb

Climb to a branch, take a bold leap,
Mischief awaits where secrets creep.
A daring squirrel makes a scene,
Shuffling leaves, a playful routine.

With every twitch and twitchy tail,
They spin and twirl, they never fail.
Oh, look at me! I'm the king!
In this little world, let laughter ring.

Why worry on and fret in vain?
When joy can come from a tiny grain.
So join the games, embrace the cheer,
The world's a stage, and fun is near.

From lofty heights to garden beds,
Nature laughs, and worries shed.
So take a cue, let worries fly,
And dance with joy 'neath the endless sky.

Mischievous Paws and Ponderings

With tiny paws and sneaky glee,
They plot and plan, so carefree.
A dash, a leap, into the grass,
Where moments twinkle, breezes pass.

Questions swirl like autumn leaves,
What's the secret that joy retrieves?
In every twitch, a tale unfolds,
Chasing dreams, or so we're told.

Oh, stop and laugh, the sun will wink,
As furry wonders make us think.
They gather stories, nuts, and joys,
Our hearts enchanted by nature's ploys.

So watch them dance and sway with grace,
These furry friends in this vast space.
With each pitter-patter, life shines bright,
A playful romp, a pure delight.

Adventures in the Smallest of Things

Amidst the grass, a hero stands,
In search of treasures not in plans.
They scurry forth with a cheeky grin,
Adventure calls, let the fun begin!

From tiny twigs to pebbled roads,
Each found joy, like hidden codes.
In fleeting glances, spirits soar,
The circus of life, we can't ignore.

With every leap, the world expands,
Through curious eyes and tiny hands.
So chase the giggles, skip the pain,
For joy's sweet spark is hard to feign.

So join the dance, let worries cease,
In every nut, there's boundless peace.
The tiniest wonders bring the best,
With squeaks and chirps, we're truly blessed.

Nature's Concerto at Dusk

Whispers of wind play a tune,
Crickets join in, under the moon.
A shadow darts, quick as a flash,
Oh, it's just a bushy-tailed dash.

The orchestra swells, the stars come out,
Nature's concert, no room for doubt.
Bouncing between trees with perfect flair,
What's that little critter up to? Not a care!

A Glimpse of Joy Amongst the Trees

Sunlight dances on leaves so bright,
Laughter echoes, a pure delight.
A flash of fur, mischievous and spry,
Chasing a dream, oh my, oh my!

Bouncing and leaping, without a plan,
A furry acrobat, a tiny Stan.
From branch to branch, in a playful race,
Reminds us to smile, life's a fun chase.

The Sudden Spark of Curiosity

A ripple in leaves, a rustle so sly,
What's lurking there? A surprise, oh my!
Tiny paws scurry, they seem to know,
Adventure awaits wherever they go.

Zooming past twigs, they take a chance,
Life's a party, not just a dance.
In every nook, new wonders await,
Following fun, they ignore the fate.

Unraveling Mysteries in the Grass

Underfoot whispers, secrets abound,
With the flick of a tail, joy can be found.
Searching for snacks in the soft green blades,
Finding small treasures, none ever fades.

Each nibble, each leap, a new little thrill,
Searching for acorns is quite a skill.
Abundant laughter in sunlit displays,
Even nature's critters brighten our days.

Chasing Shadows in the Twilight

In the dusk, we run and play,
Chasing shadows that slip away.
A flicker, a rustle, a sudden pause,
What's that? A squirrel with shiny claws!

Giggles echo through the trees,
As we trip on roots and catch a breeze.
The world's so wild, eccentric, expanding,
Moments like these are truly demanding!

We ponder why we twirl and spin,
The answer's lost in a cheeky grin.
Laughter bubbles, and hearts feel light,
Squirrels dance in fading light!

A jump, a leap, oh, what's next?
A mystery, a riddle, we feel perplexed.
The chase resumes with happy shouts,
As joy erupts and fear falls out!

Whispers of the Unexpected

Up in the branches, whispers swirl,
A twitching tail gives me a twirl.
What secrets do those small paws keep?
A hint of mischief before I sleep!

Fleeting shadows, swift as thought,
In a game of tag, they've surely caught.
With every scurry and every squeak,
They weave a tale, oh so unique!

The trees erupt in gleeful cheer,
As tiny acrobats draw near.
Whimsical wonders, silly and bold,
In moments like these, our hearts unfold!

So let us laugh in the fading light,
For whispers of joy keep spirits bright.
A squirrel's flicker, a playful dash,
In the dance of life, we find the flash!

The Dance of the Everyday

In drizzles of dawn, the world wakes slow,
With twinkling eyes, bright as a show.
A squirrel pirouettes on a branch high,
Just like us, they reach for the sky!

Jumps and tumbles, a game of chance,
That little rascal knows how to dance.
Through puddles and grasses, in sunshine's glow,
Mischief unfolds in the moments we sow.

Through laughter and play, we learn to soar,
Chasing each other, wanting more.
In the everyday guise of a nutty quest,
These are the moments we cherish best!

So let's embrace the squirrel's delight,
In simple antics, we find our light.
And as the curtain of twilight draws near,
Let giggles and joy be all that we hear!

Fleeting Moments in the Meadow

In a meadow bright, we frolic and spin,
Catching the laughter that bubbles within.
A flash of fur darts past in a whirl,
Oh look, a friend! It's a bushy-tailed twirl!

With every hop and soft, gentle rustle,
We find joy in the silly and bustle.
A dash, a dive, what fun they bring,
Squirrels rejoice as we jump and sing!

Merging mundane with pure delight,
Chasing dreams that take flight in the light.
With giggles and grins beneath the vast sky,
Squirrels remind us, oh, my, oh, my!

So let's spin in circles, twirling around,
In fleeting moments, true joy is found.
With furry comrades and silly games bright,
In this playful world, everything feels right!

The Heartbeat of Serenity

In the park where laughter plays,
Grass stains and sunny rays.
A twitchy tail darts by,
Beneath the tree, oh my!

Life's quirks always catch my eye,
As I munch on pie nearby.
A rustle turns my head,
It's just a nut's homestead!

Chasing shadows, skipping stones,
Forget my thoughts, I hum with tones.
The world's a stage for a furry scene,
With thoughts more playful than serene.

The squeaky dance of bushy tails,
At times, the best of epic tales.
In every jump, delight we find,
With silly stories on our mind.

Joy in the Midst of Wanderlust

Traveling far with a little grin,
A wandering soul, where to begin?
Amidst the sights, a message clear,
Nature's jest brings much cheer.

In a forest, my heart does race,
A whiskered bandit finds its place.
With cheeks full of treasures, ever so round,
It hides and leaps without a sound.

Through cities bustling, I chase the sun,
Every step, a new chance for fun.
And behold, what's that, a furry blur?
Just a squirrel, oh how they stir!

With every giggle in this grand quest,
Little joys keep us all blessed.
In laughter and wonder, we reconnect,
Happiness found in the unexpected.

A Mosaic of Fleeting Experiences

Moments flit like dancing light,
In the park, a playful sight.
A flash of fur and teasing pounce,
Nature's jest, oh what a bounce!

Swinging high, thoughts take flight,
Chasing joy, no need for fright.
Sudden whispers rustle leaves,
A cheeky critter, my heart believes.

Glimpses shared in vibrant hues,
Capturing bliss like morning dew.
A tiny acorn in its clutch,
A moment simple, yet so much.

We weave our days with laughter bright,
A tapestry of pure delight.
In a world where giggles reign,
The silliest joys break every chain.

Whirling Thoughts in the Garden

In the garden where thoughts collide,
Whirling dervishes, side by side.
A sudden dash beneath the sun,
Oh, look—two squirrels having fun!

With tiny paws they plot and scheme,
Living life like a wacky dream.
Among the petals, joy abounds,
As laughter echoes all around.

A frolic here, a hop so spry,
As daisies nod and blossoms sigh.
It's silly, really, this dance we share,
In the company of nature, we find our flair.

From twirling minds to wayside chats,
Just playful antics of joyful spats.
We chase the whimsy, banish strife,
Thank a squirrel for this crazy life!

Nature's Unexpected Inspirations

A rustle in the leaves calls,
Bright-eyed critters dart and crawl,
With every leap and little bound,
All wisdom lost, yet joy is found.

Chasing tails and twinkling eyes,
In leaps and bounds, the heart complies,
What a jest, this fleeting dance,
Nature's riddle, a silly trance.

Forget the plans and grand designs,
As whiskered sprites steal all the signs,
In every silent, cheeky dive,
The world feels brighter, more alive.

Oh, what's that scampering around?
A fluffy fable on the ground,
With every glance, the chase returns,
In small delights, our laughter burns.

Fleeting Glimpses

A flicker of fur flits by,
How many secrets in that spry?
Chasing shadows, never knows,
If grass now hides or simply shows.

So many moments come and go,
Their fleeting glimmers start to glow,
The unexpected is quite grand,
A furry nugget close at hand.

As I pause, the world spins slow,
Where did it go? I want to know!
As giggles dance in sun's warm light,
I find my focus in such flight.

Peeking out from there to here,
This happy chaos, oh dear, oh dear!
With every leap, my heart aligns,
In silly moments, joy defines.

The Magic of the Mundane

In the yard, a treasure waits,
Beneath the tree that bends and shakes,
With tiny paws, it scurries near,
Mundane becomes the most sincere.

Leaves flutter gently, stories shared,
As all the world seems unprepared,
A minor blip in daily grind,
Yet winks of magic, we all find.

The ordinary feels so grand,
When furry visitors take a stand,
Their tiny quirks shift every thought,
In each funny leap, wisdom's caught.

Oh, look again, what's in your way?
A burst of laughter, a game to play,
In every odd and silly sight,
Lies the joy of pure delight.

Curious Hearts in Motion

What's that twitch of furry tail?
An adventurer on the trail,
Curious spark in keen pursuit,
Searching for crumbs—oh, how astute!

Through brambles thick, the journey's made,
Each little hop, a grand parade,
With whiskers twitching, sights are set,
To puzzle through the grand vignette.

As giggles rise with every chase,
Tiny beings, the silliest grace,
In comic turns, their antics play,
Illuminate the dullest day.

Oh, the joy in watching them roam,
Each dash and dart brings laughter home,
In the dance of daylight's glee,
Curious hearts, wild and free.

Discoveries in the Garden of Life

In the garden where laughter sprouts,
Tiny critters play, there's no doubt.
Butterflies dance, a silly parade,
While ants march on, quite unafraid.

Worms wiggle in dirt, a squishy delight,
Chasing the shadows, in morning light.
A dandelion smiles, a weed or a prize?
Who knew such joys lurked right under our eyes?

Tossing away worries, let's sit for a snack,
While squirrels debate how to stash what they lack.
With nutty ambitions, they ponder and plot,
In their busy little world, they forget what is not.

A blooming surprise, sweet moments embrace,
With giggles and whispers, we quicken our pace.
In the garden, we find treasures galore,
Such silly distractions keep us wanting more.

The Charm of Unexpected Visitors

A flash of fur and a wiggle of tail,
An unexpected guest, never too frail.
With a curious glance and a playful dash,
A rendezvous starts with a little clash.

The doorbell rings, not quite what we thought,
A squirrel in a hat, having fun, overwrought.
"Care for a snack?" it chattered with glee,
While I stood there amazed, should I offer tea?

It danced on the porch with a charming flair,
Spinning in circles, without any care.
A mix of confusion, joy in the air,
Who knew life's surprises could be so rare?

So I'll raise a toast with my new furry friend,
To odd encounters that twist and bend.
In moments of madness, we often find gold,
In the charm of the unexpected, true joy unfolds.

Revelry in the Ordinary

A cup of coffee, a soft morning light,
Fluffy clouds dance, a mesmerizing sight.
With crumbs on my shirt and hair in disarray,
I laugh at my antics, come what may.

Outside my window, the world spins around,
A squirrel on a mission, a treasure is found.
It scrambles and scampers, a nut to secure,
While I sip my brew, life feels so pure.

With mundane magic, I make my own fun,
In the warmth of the sun, where laughter's begun.
The rhythm of chaos, a song from the pines,
Reminds me of joys that need no design.

So let's dance in the kitchen, let mess be the law,
When revelry calls, we answer with awe.
For in every heartbeat, the ordinary sings,
And life's little quirks are the best of all things.

The Joys of Wandering Thoughts

My mind wanders freely, quite eager to play,
Drifting like leaves in a breezy display.
I ponder the wonders of clouds up above,
Then—oh look, a squirrel! It's full of sweet love.

It leaps over branches, a curious sprite,
Dancing through shadows, a whimsical sight.
On a quest for some acorns, full of such glee,
A burst of delight that's infectious to see.

I drift through my day, from one thought to next,
Caught up in giggles, my mind is perplexed.
From pondering life to the snack I forgot,
Squirrels remind me to cherish the spot.

A chorus of chuckles, my thoughts intertwine,
For wandering minds and a squirrel in sunshine.
In this odd little dance, joy takes a chance,
As silliness whispers, let's join in and prance.

www.ingramcontent.com/pod-product-compliance
Lightning Source LLC
Chambersburg PA
CBHW051701160426
43209CB00004B/978